# DID NOT SINK

Misadventures in Running, Cycling and Swimming
(Book Four in the DNF Series)

George Mahood

Copyright © 2021 by George Mahood

All rights reserved. This book or any portion thereof may not be reproduced or used in any manner whatsoever without the express written permission of the author except for the use of brief quotations in a book review.

This edition published 2021 by George Mahood.

www.facebook.com/georgemahood
www.instagram.com/georgemahood
www.twitter.com/georgemahood
www.georgemahood.com

# ONE

Never did I expect that a silicone swim hat could hold such significant power over me.

The previous year, my friends Matt and Charlie had sent me a reminder the day before entry opened for the Dart 10k swim. It sells out very quickly and they wanted to make sure I remembered. Having completed the swim once before, I had no desire to do it again so politely declined. This year they didn't remind me it was open for entries, assuming I would once again have no interest. Matt and Charlie would both soon be given a gold swim hat – awarded to those who swim the Dart 10k three times. Little did they know that not only had I remembered it was sign up day, but I had registered for the swim twice. This year I would be taking part on both the Saturday and the Sunday.

I bumped into Matt one cold morning at a local beach.

'I'm all signed up for the Dart 10k again in September,' he said smugly. 'Can't wait to show off my gold swim hat. You're going to be so jealous.'

'Nah, I won't be jealous, mate. Because I'll have one

too.'

'Have you signed up this year?'

'Yes.'

'Nice one. I thought you were never doing it again? So, you'll be able to get your gold swim hat next year.'

'No, I'll be getting my gold swim hat this year.'

'Er, no, mate, I'm afraid you have to do it THREE times to get your gold hat.'

'I know. This year I am swimming it twice.'

'Ha, very funny,' laughed Matt, before realising I wasn't smiling. 'Err, what do you mean you're swimming it twice?'

'I'm doing it on the Saturday AND the Sunday.'

'Wait... WHAT? WHY? I don't understand.'

'To get my gold hat, of course. I can't have you prancing around town with your gold hat and a smug look on your face.'

Matt laughed then stood there opened-mouthed, shaking his head at me in disbelief.

'Oh. My. God. You're serious, aren't you? You're really going to swim it twice?'

'Absolutely.'

'I can't believe you've done that. All for a gold swim hat? You are such a dick.'

'It seemed like a good idea at the time. But I'm already regretting it. I mean, I hated it last time. Imagine what's it's going to be like doing it twice in a weekend.'

'You're completely insane. I can't wait to tell Charlie. He'll think you're mental.'

I sent my friend Emily a message telling her I had signed up twice and that I was going to be getting my gold swim hat. Emily had also swum the Dart 10k just once before. She replied with exactly what I expected.

'I've just signed up for it twice, too.'

# TWO

During the previous year's Exeter Marathon, I had been unable to keep up with Rachel and she went on to achieve her Good for Age time. Since then, I had tried to rekindle my relationship with running and increase my mileage. I wasn't following any sort of training plan, but it felt like I was getting a little fitter and a little faster. With this year's Exeter Marathon approaching, I should have been preparing to try for a new PB but decided against it. My sciatica was particularly bad – possibly aggravated by my increased running – and although my fitness had improved, I was unable to run without a significant amount of pain and discomfort. Also, my friend Simon had asked if I would run with him to help him try to break 4 hours for the first time. I told him I would be very happy to run with him, but also warned him that I had only broken 4 hours twice in my previous ten marathons.

'So, Simon,' I said, a couple of days before the Exeter Marathon. 'Are you planning on sticking to a steady 9 minutes per mile for the whole marathon?'

'No. I've got a strict plan in place. It's fool proof.'

'Cool, let me hear it.'

'Ok, so we will start off running at just under 8.30-minute mile pace.'

'That's quite quick, but go on.'

'So, we do that for the first nine miles, and then we drop to 9-minute miles from miles 9 to 18. And then we do the final eight at 9.30. That should get us in under 4 hours. What do you think?'

'Yeah, it could work. It's quite ambitious. 8.30 is faster than most of your training runs, so you might find you're knackered before halfway.'

'But we only have to keep up that pace for the first nine miles.'

'Nine miles is still quite a long way.'

'I think it will work. There's only one way to find out.'

Rachel had deferred her Exeter Marathon place this year as it was only a couple of weeks after her London Marathon, and she had a few niggles that she didn't want to exacerbate.

Our friend Ross was also running Exeter. This was his first ever marathon. Ross was not as fixated on the sub-4-hour marathon as Simon, but he decided to start with us and see how he got on.

Simon was on a mission from the moment the starting pistol sounded and set off at a pace even faster than the one he had planned.

At about the 5-mile point, Ross said he needed to stop for a wee.

'We'll slow down and wait for you to catch up, won't we, Simon?' I said.

Simon glanced at his watch. He was in the zone.

'Yep, can do,' said Simon.

'No, it's fine,' said Ross. 'You guys go on. This pace is a bit too fast for me anyway.'

'It's a bit too fast for me too!' I whispered.

'Good luck, guys. See you at the finish,' said Ross.

'Good luck, mate,' said Simon.

'Another four miles at this pace and then we can slow the pace slightly,' said Simon, sounding a little fatigued for the first time.

I glanced at my watch, noticing we had slowed slightly already.

'We might not have a choice about when we slow down,' I said.

'What do you mean?'

'I mean that our bodies might decide to slow down before your race plan says we are allowed to.'

'Well, we will just have to push through. We can't slow until we get to the 9-mile marker.'

Simon uses a unique series of techniques to help keep his mind focused during endurance events.

For the half-Ironman swim, he broke down his swim into sections, with each one representing a colour of the rainbow. A certain number of strokes would complete that colour and then he would move onto the next one. So rather than becoming overwhelmed by the big picture, the event is broken down into manageable chunks, or colours of a rainbow.

For the Exeter Marathon, Simon imagined an empty pie dish. The dish had space for eight slices of pie. Every half an hour, Simon could add a new slice of pie to the dish. But this wasn't just any old pie, this pie was magic and could be made up of whatever combination of slices you wanted – sweet, savoury, cheesy, spicy, hot or cold. The possibilities were endless.

The idea is to break down the marathon into half hour chunks, and also keep your brain occupied with deciding on the flavour of the pie, depending on how you feel at the time, but also rewarding the brain with a slice of imaginary pie.

Writing this down, I realise an imaginary slice of pie doesn't seem like much in the way of a reward. But it works for Simon, and his techniques helped get him through both his half-Ironman and our Dartmoor Way bike ride.

I loved the idea and became fully absorbed in creating my own pie as we ran. We filled a lot of the time with conversation and debate about whose pie was better. It's always savoury foods that I crave while running, so I dismissed Simon's controversial slice of key lime pie that he introduced at the 10-mile point, opting for a slice of steak and ale pie instead. The trouble was, the more I thought about pies, the hungrier I became, and this visualisation technique became a form of mental torture for me.

Our speed dropped considerably soon after we passed halfway, and I think Simon and I both knew that the chance of breaking 4 hours was rapidly fading. I had been asked to pace him, so felt it was my duty to try and encourage him to speed up a little.

'I'll try. Is this better?' he said, quickening his step slightly.

'Yeah, I think so. How are you feeling?'

'Not too good.'

'Maybe you should have another of your gels.'

'I don't think I can face another gel yet.'

'What slice pie are you planning next?'

'I'm torn between chicken and mushroom or cheese and onion.'

'Tough call. I could eat both of those now.'

I pulled out a packet of salt and vinegar Hula Hoops (other ringed potato snacks are available, just not as good). These had become my secret weapon during endurance events.

'Here, Simon. Try one of these.'

'No thanks. I definitely couldn't eat crisps now.'

'Honestly, try one, you won't regret it.'

He fumbled with the packet and put a single Hula Hoop into his mouth.

'Holy SHIT! Oh my god, that's incredible!'

'See! I told you they were good. Want another?'

'Yes please!'

There is something about the extreme saltiness that floods the senses, and almost gives you a gentle slap around the face. Logic would imply that salty crisps would suck all the moisture from your mouth, leaving you desperate for water. But instead, the sharpness of the vinegar stimulates saliva production, leaving you not only nourished, but somehow feeling re-hydrated too. Look at me, analysing a Hula Hoop as though it's some fine-dining experience. But seriously, if you're planning some long physical challenge, take a packet of salt and vinegar Hula Hoops with you. You can thank me later.

At about the 19-mile point, I saw a familiar runner up ahead. I had chatted to Ruth at each of the Cornish Marathons I had run, as well as at the Exeter Marathon a year earlier. Ruth was in her 50s and had completed almost 600 marathons. She finished her first one in 2002, with no training and suffering a horrendous hangover. She then did another, and another, and has averaged about three a month since that first one.

The fascinating thing about Ruth, which defies all logic, is that she genuinely hates running. She often finishes last in her races, sometimes taking well over six hours to complete the course and finds the running process incredibly tough and tedious. But then she'll soon be back out there again (often the next day) to take on another marathon.

Ruth is always recognisable because of the brightly patterned leggings she runs in. She was down to a slow walk, and as some sections of the Exeter Marathon are repeated loops, I estimated she was about six miles behind us.

'Hi Ruth,' I said, as we ran alongside her. 'How are you doing?'

Ruth didn't know my name, but I had chatted to her enough times at events that I think she recognised my face.

'Oh hi,' she said, her head only lifting briefly. 'It's going to be a bit of a slog this one.'

'It'll soon be over. When is your next one? Will you get to have a break?'

'My next one is tomorrow.'

'Oh, wow. Do you ever want to just take a break from marathons?'

'All the time. I mean, does it look like I'm enjoying myself?'

'No, not really. But you always seem so happy when I've seen you before and after marathons.'

'Oh, those are the bits I love. It's the whole community aspect that keeps me signing up for more.'

'Have you got many more lined up?'

'I think I'm already signed up for another 40.'

'40? Wow, that's amazing.'

'It's a bit annoying because I've now got this obligation that I can't really escape from.'

'Well, I think you're really inspiring.'

'Thank you. Don't let me hold you up. Thanks for chatting. Well done, both of you.'

'Great to chat to you again, Ruth. Enjoy the rest of your run.'

'I'll try.'


Simon would have happily munched through the entire bag of Hula Hoops, but we still had a long way to go.

'Use them to reward me,' he said. 'You keep running and I'll just follow the Hula Hoops. Like the donkey and carrot technique.'

Speech soon became too much of a challenge, so Simon developed a specific look that he gave me to indicate he required another Hula Hoop. It was a subtle nod of the head, accompanied by a not so subtle 'num num' sound. Thankfully, I had brought two packets, so had enough to entice him all the way to the finish.

I had also managed to squeeze a couple of cheese sandwiches into my running belt. Simon declined my offer – opting for his gels instead – but I munched my way through both during the course of the 26.2 miles.

Unfortunately, neither the Hula Hoops nor cheese sandwiches could save our pace, which was rapidly plummeting. We could still break 4 hours, but going by my calculations, it would require us to run the final 10k faster than we ran the first. And we both knew this wasn't going to happen.

It was at about the 21-mile mark that Simon's tears first began to flow. One minute he was chatting away normally, the next, his entire face screwed up tightly and he began sobbing uncontrollably. He pulled his sunglasses down from his forehead to cover his eyes and cried for about thirty seconds as we continued running. Then, as quickly as they started, the tears stopped.

'Ok,' he said, surprisingly jovially, lifting his sunglasses back up to the top of his head. 'Sorry about that. I feel much better now.'

'Shit, mate. Are you alright?'

'Yep, I feel great now. I think I just needed to get that out of my system.'

'You had me worried for a while.'

'It happened a few times in the Cotswolds half-Ironman too. You saw what I was like when I crossed the finish line of that one. Sometimes I just get overwhelmed by it all.'

A couple of miles later, it happened to Simon again. This time, rather than watching or feeling too concerned, I let him be, and thirty seconds later he was back to normal again.

It had happened to me a few times before – mostly memorably during my Ironman – but on each of those occasions, there had been a gradual build-up, and then a slow recovery after the tears. I was in awe of Simon's ability to rapidly transition between extreme emotions.

As his pacer, part of me felt guilty and responsible for Simon not achieving his sub-4-hour marathon. But it's not as if I had been his personal trainer. We did go for occasional runs together, but they were always social rather than me offering any help or advice to improve his fitness. Not that I would know how to help or advise someone even if they wanted me to. But the other – perhaps bigger – part of me was relieved that the pressure of the sub-4-hour marathon had passed. I probably could have scraped round in under 4 hours, but it would have been a struggle. My sciatica was worse than ever and would have only been exacerbated by maintaining a quicker pace for the duration. Slowing down had relieved some of the pain, and also removed all of the pressure.

Up ahead, a group of boy scouts were standing on the edge of the path, clapping, cheering, and offering high-fives as we passed.

'Wasn't that lovely,' said Simon, but the 'lovely' became choked up in tears. He flicked his sunglasses down again.

'Nearly there, mate. You've done brilliantly. What flavour pie are you on now?'

'Oh, I don't care about the stupid fucking pie anymore,' he laughed.

Simon had run his first marathon twenty years previously and then didn't run another in the following twenty years. His goals and dreams had all been about breaking the elusive 4-hour mark. But he was missing out on all the positives. He was still on for a PB. That meant that as a man now in his mid-forties, he was fitter than he had been in his twenties. That was surely something to celebrate.

'What was your first London marathon time again?' I said.

'4 hours and 17 minutes.'

'You're going to smash that, mate. This will be a massive PB for you. You should be very proud. Your sub four-hour will come soon.'

With the spectators now a little less sporadic as we approached the finish line, we both increased the pace slightly and mustered a fast finish. With 100 metres to go, Simon's sunglasses came down once again and we crossed the line in 4h 13m.

Ross finished strongly a little while later. The pace of the first 10k had been too much for him (and me and Simon) and the rest of the marathon had been a struggle, but he was delighted to have completed his first marathon.

Simon felt very despondent after the race. He had been fixated with achieving a sub-4-hour marathon, and it had been a dream that disappeared for him fairly early in the race. I kept reminding him about his PB, but it didn't seem to be any consolation.

He didn't dwell on it for too long, however. Later that

evening, he sent me a message saying he had worked out what had gone wrong and adapted his training plan. The hunt for sub four was back on.

A few weeks later, Rachel, Simon and I – plus three other friends – travelled up to the Cotswolds to take part in the Cotswold 113 half-Ironman again. Rachel had been looking forward to it since crossing the finish line the previous year, Simon had signed up straight away after bawling his way across the finish line and swearing he would never do it again, and our friends Ross, Claire and Kate were all first-timers.

Having learned the lesson the hard way the year before, I remembered to put on my tri-suit the correct way this time, and it was another fantastic – and much less stressful – day. Ross, Claire and Kate all did brilliantly and loved the experience of their first middle-distance triathlon. Simon crossed the line without tears and a big smile on his face. I was seven minutes slower overall than the previous year, but Rachel improved her time by 10 minutes. I still beat her (get in!), but the gap was closing.

# THREE

After chatting to me about last year's Dartmoor Classic, my good friend James was eager to take part in this year's event with me. I realise it might be confusing reading about different mentions of the Dartmoor Classic, Dartmoor Ways, Dart 10ks, Dartington Duathlon, Dart Dart Dart... The Dartmoor Classic is the organised cycling sportive that I had taken part in the previous year with Rachel and Marta. The one where we were racing the old lady.

Despite the tears and tantrums the previous year, Rachel signed up again for the 110-mile Grande route. Daniel, Marta and their three children had sadly moved back to Spain. This wasn't because they didn't enjoy life in England. They had planned to come to Devon for two years to have an adventure and allow their children to learn English. They ended up staying for three. We were really sad to say goodbye but knew it would not be the last we saw of them. Rachel persuaded her friend Claire to sign up to the Dartmoor Classic, too. Claire, like Rachel the previous year, had never cycled further than 56 flat miles before, so would be taking on her first century bike ride in style.

Depending on which weather forecast we checked, the outlook varied from extreme rain to tropical heat – so we were in for an unpredictable day. The previous year's event had been dry, but that was a rarity for Dartmoor. There is a local saying that goes something like, *'If you can't see Dartmoor, it means it is raining. If you can see Dartmoor, it is about to rain.'*

We arrived at the start at Newton Abbot Racecourse to bright blue sky and what promised to be a glorious day. James and I foolishly opted to just wear t-shirts (and a pair of cycling shorts, obviously). Rachel and Claire even more naively opted to wear running vests.

James is an experienced cyclist having been on several cycling holidays in the Alps. He was much fitter and faster than I was, but he had come down to Devon from Birmingham to cycle the Classic with me, so I knew (or at least hoped) he would be happy to go at my pace. After the frustration Rachel felt at cycling with Marta and me the previous year, I tried to subtly suggest to her that perhaps we should not all cycle together this time.

'It's alright, George, I get it!' she said. 'Claire and I don't want to cycle with you and James either.'

'It's not that I don't want to cycle with you. It's that I think we'll probably be going a bit faster this year. I will struggle to keep up with James, and if... I... er...'

'And if YOU are struggling to keep up with James, then

there is no chance that I will keep up? Is that what you're saying?'

'Well... er... no, not exactly. It's just...'

'I'm joking! You're right. Of course I wouldn't be able to keep up. It's honestly fine. I really don't want to cycle with you two. Claire and I are really looking forward to cycling together.'

The first twenty miles were great fun. Well, as fun as cycling up big hills on Dartmoor can be, as James and I cycled through Bovey Tracey then up onto the moor. The Strava *King of the Mountains* segment up Beckaford Hill came into view. This was the climb I had busted myself up the previous year, only to accidentally stop long before the official finish and in the end be beaten by both Rachel and Marta. This year I decided not to humiliate myself in front of James, so switched into the granny gear and took it steady all the way up. As we emerged onto the open moor at the top, Dartmoor was showing off her full beauty and I felt strangely proud.

'Not a bad view, hey?' I said.

'It's stunning,' said James. 'I thought Dartmoor was just going to be a load of hills and grass. This is incredible.'

'That's what I thought for the first 35 years of my life. Although, I suppose it is basically a load of hills and grass, but they are incredibly beautiful hills and grass.'

Dartmoor showed her dark side ten minutes later. We should have paid more attention to the local saying about the weather. Because we could see Dartmoor, it meant it was about to rain. The wind suddenly picked up and the rain came down theatrically. We were soaked through within minutes; the roads became treacherous, and it didn't relent for the next five hours. Rachel and I used to mock the dramatic narration in TV documentaries or survival shows when the presenter (usually Bear Grylls) explained how '*out here, conditions can deteriorate in an instant. I'm standing in this dried-up riverbed, but a FLASH FLOOD could appear any second and wash me away.*'

'*No, it won't, Bear!*' we would say. '*Surely you'd get a bit of warning – the sky clouds over, maybe a bit of light drizzle first or even a clap of thunder. Don't be so dramatic. You're not going to get washed away.*'

Well, it turns out Bear Grylls had a point. The weather can deteriorate in an instant. There was no warning or gradual change of conditions whatsoever. One minute there was bright sun and blue sky, the next it felt like we were cycling through a car wash.

On the long, slow uphills, the rain wasn't too problematic as we were kept warm from the exertion of pedalling. On the long, fast downhills, however, it was a different story. The water rushed down these roads more than an inch deep. Using the brakes was essential but treacherous, and because there was no need to pedal and our clothes were soaked through, we suddenly felt bitterly cold.

I started to think about Rachel. Not only did she hate

cycling in the rain, but she is petrified of wet roads and fast downhills. She also tends to feel the cold a lot more than I do and was cycling in just a running vest.

James and I made it to the first feed station at Princetown, where visions of lazing on the grass with a plate of food like previous years were somewhat hampered by the torrential rain. Instead, I went to the portable toilet and lingered much longer than is normal, for the simple reason that it provided shelter.

We wolfed down a few sandwiches, crisps and cake, and returned to our bikes. I had hoped that Rachel and Claire would have appeared at the feed station before we left as it would have been nice to know they were doing ok. I felt really guilty for not cycling with them; although, I could not have done anything to change the situation. I hoped they were alright and would perhaps be able to find some enjoyment from the experience.

Just after the feed station, we came to the junction where there was an option to turn left and follow the shorter Medio route back to the finish. Perhaps Rachel and Claire would turn left here. A ride of 68 miles in these conditions would be more than enough. If James hadn't come all the way down from Birmingham, it is very likely I would have turned left.

The following few miles made us both wish we had. From Princetown, the road descended fast off the moor down towards Tavistock on the western edge of Dartmoor. The previous year, this had been one of the most enjoyable sections of the entire ride; several miles with only the occasional need to pedal, the air cooling the riders during a hot July day. It had been a chance to savour the moment, take in the scenery and give the legs a rest. Today, however, it was the most unpleasant section by far. Our clothes, which had been drenched through for a couple of hours, stuck tight to our bodies in the bitter wind. With no need to pedal, the cold soon permeated every limb, and we cursed our stupid decision to wear short-sleeved t-shirts. Our hands, only partially functioning, were required to apply the brakes constantly because of the sheets of water that were rushing down the road. I'm a fair-weather cyclist and have very little experience of cycling in the rain, and I found it a difficult balancing act deciding how much to apply the brakes, not wanting to go so fast that I lost control, but also resisting using them too much and risk skidding off the road. I let James set both the pace and the line and tried my best to keep up with him. He would occasionally look back over his shoulder to check I was ok and shout some instructions to me, but I hoped what he was saying was not too important, as each time he spoke his words disappeared into the wind.

What made the whole situation infinitely worse was that however difficult I was finding it, and however much I hated the conditions, I knew that Rachel was likely hating it even more. She's not a fan of cycling downhill even in dry weather, so this would be her worst nightmare. All I could do was hope she turned left. She would be annoyed with herself for not completing the full loop, but James and I could reassure her later that she had made the right decision.

The weather eased slightly from about 60 miles, and after we hit the long uphill sections back up to Princetown, we began to warm up a little. Although it was several hours later before feeling returned to our fingers and toes.

When we arrived at the feed station for the second time, I took my phone out of my bike bag to see if I had any messages from Rachel. Despite being a waterproof phone which I had wrapped in a sandwich bag (just in case), the phone had succumbed to the weather and the screen was blank. My GPS watch, which was supposedly suitable for swimming, stopped working completely. It turned out it was waterproof enough for swimming, but not suitable for the kind of wetness you get after a day on Dartmoor.

My phone did eventually recover after a few days sitting in a bowl of rice. My watch never did.

I had been a little apprehensive about cycling with James for the day. I knew he was a much stronger cyclist, and I didn't want to feel like I was holding him back. But the weather acted as a bit of a leveller, and we made an excellent team. It became clear that I am not the easiest person to cycle with, however. I have quite an erratic style, and it's almost impossible to draft behind me. Because of ongoing discomfort while riding my bike, I alternate regularly between seated and standing positions, which therefore results in extreme fluctuations in speed. James has a much more measured (some might say, better) style and maintains a consistent pace.

With about 15 miles of the race to go, most of which were downhill and then flat, we realised there was a chance we might finish inside the cut-off for a silver medal, which, considering the conditions, would be an impressive achievement. I hadn't even considered being fast enough for a silver medal in dry conditions and had only thoughts of completing the course. The rain finally stopped, the wind dropped, and the sun made fleeting appearances from behind the clouds. With the prospect of a silver medal now on the cards, it became an added incentive to push harder for those final few miles.

And then, just as I dug deep to try for a strong finish, I felt the back wheel wobble slightly as I went around a corner and the familiar rubbing noise that indicated a flat tyre. I looked down, hoping that maybe it was just paranoia, but could see the rear tyre splayed out on the road surface.

'Sorry, James,' I shouted, pulling over on the side of the road. 'I've got a flat.'

'Ah, bugger, that's bad timing. Just when things were starting to get easier.'

'I know. Sorry, why don't you go on ahead? You might as well get the silver medal while you can.'

'No, don't be silly. I'm not bothered about the medal.

Have you got a spare tube?'

'Yeah, I won't be too long.'

I had everything I needed and had soon replaced the tube and reattached the wheel to my bike in a Formula 1 style pit stop. For my Ironman, I had bought a couple of $CO_2$ cannisters to save on time and weight in case of a flat. I had never used them, and they had remained in my saddlebag. Now was their moment. I was just about to screw the canister onto the fitting when a motorbike screeched to a halt alongside us. It was one of the Dartmoor Classic's mobile mechanics.

'Everything ok?' he asked.

'Yep, all sorted thanks. Just had a flat tyre. Just about to inflate the new tube.'

'Is that a new $CO_2$?'

'Yes.'

He climbed off his motorbike and swaggered over like he had just ridden in on horseback.

'Don't waste your new canister. I've got one here ready to go.'

'Are you sure? That's kind, thanks.'

'No problem.'

He took charge, putting the canister onto the valve and letting out a big hiss of air. The canister, that is, not the mechanic.

'There you are. Good to go,' he said.

'Thank you. That's much appreciated.'

I gave the tyre a squeeze. It still felt very soft.

'Is that enough air do you think?'

He gave it a squeeze.

'Yeah, that should be plenty to get you to the finish.'

James gave it a squeeze too and gave me a questioning look.

'Right, well, thanks very much for your help,' I said. 'I really appreciate it.'

'No problem at all,' he said, and he climbed back onto his motorbike. I didn't want to offend him by using my own $CO_2$ canister to put a proper amount of air into the tyre while he was still there, so decided to wait until he had left.

'Thanks again,' I said, offering a cheery wave in the hope it would encourage him to drive off.

'I'll just watch and make sure you get going again ok,' he said.

'Oh, alright.'

James and I climbed onto our bikes, waited for a gap between groups of cyclists, then clipped in and re-joined the road. A few seconds later, the motorbike mechanic overtook, giving us a big thumbs up as he passed.

'How's the tyre, George?' said James from behind. 'Looks pretty soft from here.'

'It's really soft. Do you mind if I stop and put some more air into it?'

'Not at all.'

We pulled over into a lay-by and I climbed off my bike

again.

'I've got a pretty decent hand pump, if you like,' said James. 'Save your cannister.'

'Great, thanks. Why was that mechanic so stingy with his air?'

'I've no idea,' he said as he pulled a pump from the back pocket of his cycling top.

'It's like he was rationing it.'

'I can't believe you've kept your dust caps,' said James, unscrewing the black plastic cap and flinging it into a roadside bin.

'What the fuck? What did you do that for?'

'You don't need dust caps,' he smiled. 'They are just unnecessary weight.'

'Unnecessary weight? They weigh almost nothing.'

'They don't serve any purpose. They make tyre changes much slower. No proper cyclists use dust caps.'

'Yet you haven't commented on my wheel reflectors or my bike bell.'

'I'm trying hard not to look at those. They are making me rage inside.'

'You cyclists are such dicks.'

With the tyre now properly inflated, we set off to cycle the final ten miles to the finish. I felt a little guilty after causing us to miss out on a silver medal, but James didn't seem to be bothered and the puncture could just have easily happened to him. Now that the rain had stopped, it was obvious that the road was littered with sticks and stones, washed from the verges by the rainwater. There were several other cyclists fixing punctures at the roadside, and for their sake we hoped they did not receive any assistance from the mobile mechanic.

We turned the corner into Newton Abbot Racecourse and crossed the finish line in a time of 8h 09m, which was over 1h 40m faster than my previous attempt at the Grande route the year before. Considering the weather and the puncture, this felt like a massive achievement for me. After being marked down as *Did Not Start* in last year's race, this was a dramatic improvement.

On checking the results later, I discovered that out of 582 riders, James and I were 424th and 425th, which brought me back down to earth pretty quickly. The fastest rider finished in an astonishing time of 5h 35m – over 2.5 hours quicker than us.

I looked around for Rachel and Claire, half expecting – and maybe hoping – to see them somewhere at the finish. It sounds weird to be wishing a DNF on them, but the conditions were so horrendous that I didn't see how Rachel and Claire could have got any enjoyment at all from the day. I checked my phone, but the screen was still blank.

We waited another hour and there was still no sign of them, so I spoke to the officials at the results desk.

'According to this, they passed through the timing check at the Princetown feed station a little over an hour ago.'

'So they are still going? She's ok?'

'Well, yes, there's nothing to suggest otherwise.'

'That's brilliant news. Thanks very much.'

Now that the weather had improved, I was no longer worried for Rachel and Claire. They were over the worst of it and were hopefully on their final few miles back to the finish.

Fortunately, the race goodie bag contained a nice t-shirt, so James and I could change out of our wet t-shirts. We sat on the concrete floor of the racecourse grandstand, watching as the occasional cyclist came into view, each time disappointed it wasn't Rachel or Claire.

There had been a live band playing on a stage halfway along the finishing straight, but they played their final song to an audience of just James and me, and then packed up their equipment and left. The event staff began removing the barriers that lined the finishing chute.

'How do you think Rachel will feel when they finish?' asked James.

'I've no idea. Relieved, I guess. I'm so glad there are two of them. Hopefully that will have made it a little less miserable.'

'Is that them?'

I looked up, and in the distance could see the familiar running vests of Rachel and Claire cycling alongside each other. James and I stood to our feet and began cheering. The staff packing away the barriers paused and clapped too. As they neared the line, both of them were smiling and laughing hysterically. I ran along to meet them at the other side of the finish line and gave Rachel a big hug as she came to a stop.

'Oh. My. God,' she said.

'You're alive! I was so worried about you. Well done, both of you. How did you find it?'

Rachel and Claire looked at each other and burst out laughing again.

'It was... it was... a little... er... eventful,' she said.

'What happened? I'm amazed you kept going. Were you not tempted to turn left after the first aid station and do the shorter route?'

'VERY tempted. But I told Claire the next few miles to Tavistock were all downhill.'

'Oh no. That was the worst bit, wasn't it? It was so cold.'

'I honestly thought I was going to die of hypothermia,' said Claire. 'It was SO cold. But we bought some bin bags to warm us up, didn't we, Rachel?'

'Bin bags?' I said.

'Yes,' laughed Rachel. 'We called into a shop in one of those little villages near Tavistock and tried to buy a couple of waterproof coats, but they didn't sell any.'

'So Rachel asked the lady if she could possibly spare a couple of bin bags instead.'

'But the mean lady wouldn't give us any, so we had to buy a whole roll.'

'A whole roll? What did you do with the rest?'

'We gave them back to her,' said Rachel.

'And did you cycle in the bin bags?'

They both burst out laughing again.

'Yes!' said Claire. 'For about 40 miles!'

During my penniless Land's End to John O'Groats bike ride (see *Free Country: A Penniless Adventure the Length of Britain*), my friend Ben and I also acquired bin bags to cycle in. So I could appreciate their effectiveness. But 40 miles during a proper sportive is a different level of eccentricity.

'You cycled in bin bags for 40 miles? That's incredible. Weren't they flapping everywhere?'

'Absolutely, but we didn't get cold again,' said Rachel. 'We got some funny looks and comments from other cyclists. Apparently bin bags are not the norm in the cycling world.'

'I got grief for using dust caps,' I said, raising my eyebrows at James.

'Oh, and both of us fell off our bikes,' said Claire nonchalantly.

'You fell off your bikes? Are you both ok?'

I pictured all of those steep, tight downhill bends on the wet roads and thought how dangerous it could have been.

'Yes, we both fell off cycling uphill and we were going so slowly we just couldn't unclip in time.'

'Well, if you're going to fall off, it's better to do it going uphill. Was that both at the same time? Synchronised falling?'

'No, different hills,' said Claire. 'I got a nice big graze on my arm from mine.'

James stood there throughout with a big smile on his face. He was seriously impressed by their determination and ingenuity.

'So, did you enjoy it?' I said to Rachel as we collected their medals and walked to the car.

'It was completely crazy, but I weirdly did sort of enjoy it. The conditions were so bad that if I had let it get to me, I would have just cried the whole way.'

'Well, I think you were both amazing. Well done.'

A few months later, endurance cyclist Mark Beaumont set an astonishing world record of cycling around the world in 79 Days. His heroic effort involved covering a mind-blowing 240 miles per day. It was such an awe-inspiring achievement, and he's a big hero of mine. One thing jumped out at me when I saw the publicity of Mark at the finish line in Paris. I looked at one of the photos of him and his bike; his custom-built, lightweight touring bike, designed to cover thousands and thousands of miles as efficiently as possible. When I zoomed in closely on the photo, he still had the dust caps on his tyre valves. I took a screenshot of the cropped photo and sent it to James.

He replied with one word:

*'Amateur.'*

# FOUR

The Bantham Swoosh is a swimming event organised by the Outdoor Swimming Society in the Avon Estuary in South Devon. It was established in 2015 following on from the success of their flagship event, the Dart 10k. At 6k, the Swoosh is a shorter and easier event than the Dart 10k, but the novelty is the 'swoosh' which refers to the fast-flowing section of the swim towards the end; the estuary narrows and the tide and current whisk you along at an impressive speed and you exit the estuary just before being sucked out to sea.

I confess I was a little cynical about the event when I first heard about it. I thought it seemed weird to pay a substantial entry fee to swim down a river estuary that is always there, that you could swim for free whenever you liked. But the same could be true for most running and cycling events, too. The roads, trails and rivers are always there. You could run or cycle the same routes anytime. And although the Avon Estuary is always there and I could swim it for free at any time, I never had.

Rivers, and especially tidal estuaries, can be very intimidating, and swimming as part of an organised event – with kayak and SUP safety support – alleviates most of the risk and therefore the fear. But the main appeal of these organised events is the atmosphere that comes with the shared sense of occasion when taking part with other people.

Since completing her second half-Ironman, Rachel was feeling more and more confident with her open water swimming. The Bantham Swoosh really appealed to her, so I signed us both up, just days before the event, and we planned to swim it together. The furthest Rachel had ever swum was the 1.2 miles of her half Ironman, so the 6k (3.7 miles) was a significant challenge.

Having signed up for the event at the last minute, neither of us had time to think or worry about the swim, which was probably for the best. But we now found ourselves sitting in the car in a dark Bantham beach car park at 5am, with 45 minutes until our bus departed, with nothing else to do but think and worry.

'What if I drown?' said Rachel.

'You won't drown.'

'But what if I do?'

'Why would you drown?'

'I might sink.'

'You won't sink.'

'It might be too tiring for me to swim all that way, and

I won't be able to do it.'

'You will be able to do it. And if you do get too tired, I think maybe you should signal for help, or swim to the shore, rather than just give up and drown.'

'I'm really scared.'

'You'll be fine. The waiting before is always the worst bit. Once we are in the water, I'm sure you'll love it. Also, the idea of swimming in a river seems much more intimidating when it's dark outside. The sun will be up soon, and everything will feel a little less scary.'

Swimmers were encouraged not to take much with them to the start as there was limited space at the bag drop, so Rachel and I boarded the bus wearing our wetsuits and carrying only a banana each.

Getting on a bus with just a wetsuit and a banana felt very bizarre.

'Remember that time your dad wore his wetsuit on the bus?' said Rachel.

'Ha, I was just thinking exactly the same thing.'

We were on a family holiday in South Devon several years earlier and came to Bantham for a swim. For a reason I can't remember, my dad was joining us later and was going to arrive in Bantham on the bus. To save time, he decided to put his wetsuit on before leaving the holiday house. He then put all his other clothes on over the top of the wetsuit.

He had failed to consider that it was a blistering hot day in the middle of August. As soon as he stepped onto the bus, he realised he had made a big mistake. But by that point it was too late. The bus then spent about an hour winding its way through tiny villages on the way to Bantham, regularly getting caught up in holiday traffic on the narrow Devon lanes.

By the time he reached Bantham, Dad was feeling rather unwell; his face a deep shade of red and his entire body soaked through with sweat as he had effectively been sitting in a sauna wearing a wetsuit and a full set of clothes for an hour.

None of us had much sympathy for him and wondered how anyone could be daft enough to board a bus in the summer wearing a wetsuit.

And here we were, many years later, boarding a bus in the summer wearing a wetsuit. Fortunately, it was 6am and there was little chance of us overheating.


The swim start in Aveton Gifford was already busy and we stood and chatted with an older couple who had come all the way from London to take part.

'We did it last year and loved it so much we've come back.'

'Fantastic. Are you just down for the day?'

'No, we've turned it into a bit of a summer holiday, and we are spending a week down here. In fact, we came and did this swim yesterday.'

'Just the two of you?'

'Yes. It was lovely.'

It seemed crazy that they would sign up for the event, drive all the way from London, and then do the swim on their own the day before. Why bother paying for the actual event? But it reinforces the buzz that is associated with mass participation events. I imagined today's swim would be a completely different experience to their solo swim the day before. Not necessarily better, just different, and I was impressed by their bravery of taking it on twice in two days. And then I remembered my upcoming double-Dart 10k and shuddered at the thought.

With a couple of minutes to go before the start, I heard a familiar voice behind us and looked up to see my friend – and Ironman Vichy companion – Emily.

Since being unable to swim before training for her first Ironman, Emily now seems to spend more time in the water than on land. She was down in Devon with some of her open-water swimming buddies from Northamptonshire to take part in the Swoosh.

I had not seen her since we had both signed up to swim the Dart 10k twice, and it was reassuring to hear she was equally nervous. But Emily has a contagious optimism and although she thought we were both insane and it was going to be incredibly tough, she also had every confidence that we would complete the double and get our gold swim hats.

The head of the estuary at Aveton Gifford is relatively shallow. On a normal tide there is not really enough water to swim, so the Bantham Swoosh is scheduled to take place on the day of a spring tide. The event starts at high water, so it takes a little while for the outgoing tide to build up momentum and for swimmers to notice its benefit.

We all stood in a huddle by the slipway.

'I'm really nervous,' said Rachel.

'Me too. But it'll be fine. I think we will enjoy it.'

'But it's three times further than I've ever swum before.'

'Try not to think about the distance. Just think of it like we are going for a nice long swim.'

'Yeah, a nice long swim that ends with me sinking and drowning.'

'You are so dramatic.'

There was a countdown to the start and all 800 swimmers walked down the ramp and waded out into the estuary. The water was only a few feet deep and with every pull stroke we made contact with the muddy bottom. It was quite congested and there was no desire to put our faces into the thick clayey water. There was also a fair amount of seaweed in those first few hundred metres, making it feel more like we were taking part in some sort of Tough Mudder event than a swim.

'This isn't what I expected,' gasped Rachel, with a look of panic on her face.

'Don't worry. They did warn us this first bit would be a bit muddy and shallow. I'm sure it will soon open up.'

There seemed little point in trying to pull ourselves through the mud, so we did a mixture of walking and breaststroke for the first few minutes until the estuary deepened.

Despite the mud and the seaweed and the shallowness, the start to the Bantham Swoosh was far more sedate and relaxed than a triathlon swim start. Organisers kept reiterating that it wasn't a race, and there was a wonderfully relaxed feel to the event, with no elbows flying waywardly into swimmers faces and none of the 'accidental' dunkings that seem to be a more common occurrence at the start of a triathlon swim.

We were soon into the open water and the soup-like river slowly transformed into crystal clear water which we would be spoiled with all the way to Bantham. Not once during the 10k of the River Dart did I see anything under the water. Admittedly, that had been after 24 hours of heavy rain, but I had not even been able to see my own hands in front of my face.

I partly blame the River Avon for my poor geographical knowledge of the British Isles. I grew up close to the River Avon in Northamptonshire. We spent our holidays by the River Avon in South Devon, having also passed the River Avon in Bristol on the drive down. I visited the River Avon on another family holiday in Dorset, and we once went on a school trip to Stratford-upon-Avon. As a child, it never occurred to me that these were all different River Avons. I assumed these places were all linked by one, very long, indecisive river. It turns out there are also many River

Avons in Canada, New Zealand and Australia, too. It was very unimaginative, considering the word 'Avon' stems from the Celtic word for river.

'What shall we name this river that runs through our town?'

'How about the River Avon?'

'But doesn't Avon just mean river?'

'Yes, and?'

'Well, you're effectively calling it the River River.'

'So? Nobody will ever notice. It might even catch on.'

I knew this stretch of the River Avon fairly well, having had regular summer holidays to Bantham when I was growing up. I had never swum the full length of the estuary, but had often walked it at low tide, so the occasional houses, distinctive trees and rocky outcrops all looked reassuringly familiar. We used to come cockle-picking in this estuary when I was a child. My mum, dad, sister and I would wade up the river from Bantham on an outgoing tide, with the water just below our knees, looking out for the tiny gold depressions in the riverbed, and then plunging our hands deep into the sand to retrieve the cockle. We would then take them home for dinner. At least, my mum and dad would. I hated eating cockles. A slimy ball of sand and grit? Nom! But searching for them was certainly memorable. As we swam through the clear turquoise water, I could make out the cockles' distinctive holes in the sandy riverbed and it helped me forget the fact we were swimming 6k.

There was plenty of space in the river after it opened up, and Rachel and I could swim side-by-side without being in anyone's way. As we were in no rush to get to the finish, we did long periods of breaststroke so we could chat and enjoy the view. A family of swans floated elegantly by, looking remarkably serene considering there were 800 strangers swimming through their habitat. We kept our distance, just in case, because SWANS CAN BREAK YOUR ARM, YOU KNOW!

The closer we got to Bantham, the more there was to see below the surface. Even in the deeper sections, it was easy to spot fish and the distinctive dark shapes of crabs as they scuttled along the estuary's sandy bottom. During previous open water swims, holding my breath for three strokes felt like a really long time and I would have to make a conscious effort not to come up for air every two. During the Bantham Swoosh, there was so much to see underwater that I tried to eke out as many strokes as possible before turning to breathe.

The only break in the pristine sand was when we swam over an old oyster farm; the black, seaweed-coated cages lurking ominously below us. Rachel and I both quickened our stroke over this section. Other than that, we were loving the experience and as we reached the beautiful old lime kiln standing proudly at the end of Stiddicombe Creek, we knew we were over halfway.

Rachel and I spent a week in Bantham with a big group of school friends soon after we finished our A-levels. About 24 of us squashed into a house that slept six. The house had an old flat-bottomed rowing boat in the garden and one day we thought it would be fun to take the boat up the estuary on an incoming tide and have an afternoon barbecue at this lime kiln. After the tide turned, we could then float back down to Bantham on the outgoing tide.

We constructed a flotilla of boats consisting of the rowing boat and about four rubber dinghies. The Bantham Harbour Master warned us that we didn't look very well prepared, but as the tide was coming in and there was no risk of us being swept out to sea, he turned a blind eye as we launched our crafts.

We had brought several gigantic bags full of barbecue equipment, beer and food, and it didn't take too long for us to drift up to the lime kiln with the tide and begin cooking our food. An hour later, we had eaten everything, cleared up, and finished all our beers. But the tide kept coming in.

We soon realised we had got our timings badly wrong, and it would be several more hours before the tide had turned and there was enough current to float us back to Bantham. We had not brought any oars or paddles as we had assumed the tide would do all the work for us.

We sat and waited patiently for another hour, but then began to get a little worried and anxious. Not because of any impending danger, as we were well above the high-tide line, but because England were playing a crucial football match that evening and we feared we might still be stranded up the estuary and miss the game.

After the tide had reached its peak and the current became slack, we launched our flotilla back into the water, hoping to be whisked back down to Bantham. However, there was a gentle south-westerly wind and we began floating further up the estuary.

So, Mark and I (the same Mark who I later travelled across America with in my book *Not Tonight, Josephine*) climbed into the waist-deep water and waded back to Bantham dragging the entire flotilla behind us. The rest of the group were keen to stay dry in the boats. It was an utterly exhausting 1.5 miles, but we made it home just in time to get to the pub for kick-off.

'You haven't drowned yet!' I said to Rachel.
'I know. I'm so pleased to still be alive.'
'You're doing really well. How are you feeling?'
'Tired but good, thanks.'
'Me too.'

Having completed a 10k swim before, I naively assumed a 6k swim would be easy. What I neglected to consider was that for almost all the 10k swim, my arms and shoulders felt like lead. The same was true during the Swoosh, but this time I only had to contend with tired arms for a mere 6k.

Swimming with Rachel made an enormous difference,

though. Having someone to chat to and share the experience with changed it from an ordeal to a surprisingly enjoyable couple of hours.

For the final two kilometres we could feel the pull of the tide, making our swimming strokes feel more effective.

As we neared the main quay in Bantham, marshals directed swimmers over to the left of the estuary to avoid all the boats and moorings in the water. It is not until these final few hundred metres that you feel the full force of the swoosh, as the estuary narrows before it joins the sea. Rather than swim this final section, Rachel and I – like many others – just lay on our backs and let the current carry us. If only swimming was always this much fun. It is the first open-water swim that I did not want to end.

On a different holiday when I was a child, we decided to have a barbecue on the other side of the estuary to Bantham. We were holidaying with another family and required four difficult trips using the same flat-bottomed rowing boat, back and forth across the river, fighting the racing current, to shuttle us all and the food and drink to the other shore.

After we were all safely on dry land, we unloaded the boat for a final time and the grownups began setting up the barbecue. After carefully laying out the coals and firelighters, we realised that between us we had forgotten to bring any matches. Surrounded only by damp seaweed, there was no hope of making our own fire.

In the end, my dad had to walk up a set of private steps

on the steep cliff side, knock on the door of a random house, and shamefully borrow some matches.

We passed the iconic Jenkins Quay, a beautiful pink thatched boathouse at the water's edge. This was where I proposed to Rachel 15 years earlier. But there was no chance to reminisce as the swoosh is at its swooshiest here and we were whisked around the last bend to be greeted by dozens of spectators on the river beach.

We swam towards the sandy shore and were helped out of the water by some smiley race marshals.

We walked up the beach, looking around for Emily. We waited a while in case of the unlikely event she was slower than us, but after another ten minutes and still no sign, we headed back to the car park.

'Wow, that was amazing,' said Rachel.

'You didn't drown!'

'I know! I did not drown. And I did not sink. I absolutely loved it.'

'I loved it too.'

'I never thought I would ever hear you say that about swimming.'

'I never thought I would say that about swimming either. It is a very strange feeling.'

When I spoke to Emily later, it turns out she had finished her Swoosh before us and then spotted Burgh Island in the distance, which sits about half a mile out to sea from Bantham beach. Burgh Island was a favourite spot of Agatha Christie, and as Emily is a big Agatha Christie fan – and apparently not content with a mere 6k swim – she couldn't resist swimming out to the island and back too.

As much as I enjoyed the Swoosh, swimming to Burgh Island and back seemed like the least appealing thing in the world at that moment. There was no doubt that Emily's mindset and attitude was perfectly suited for her upcoming Double-Dart. I still had a lot of work to do on mine.

# FIVE

The following week I received a message from my friend Nick:

'MTB on Dartmoor on Friday? I'll drive.'

I would turn 40 in less than a year, yet I had never been mountain-biking. I have owned various mountain bikes over the years and done bits of off-road bike riding. But I had never headed out on my bike with the sole purpose of cycling over terrain that doesn't look fit for bicycles. Even my trips with the family to the off-road trails at Haldon Forest had been attempted on my road bike.

'I'd love to!' I replied. '... but I don't have a mountain bike.'

'I've got one you can borrow,' replied Nick.

A couple of days later, Nick and I drove up onto Dartmoor in his van and parked in a car park below Hound Tor – one of the most popular spots on Dartmoor. Legend has it that the rock formations of Hound Tor were formed when a local huntsman named Bowerman and his pack of dogs accidentally disturbed a witches' coven on the moor.

As punishment, the witches turned the huntsman and his dogs to stone. The weathered nearby granite stack of Bowerman's Nose – about a mile from Hound Tor – is said to be what remains of Bowerman, and it bears a remarkable resemblance to a figure. The rock formations of Hound Tor are what became of Bowerman's dogs. They bear no resemblance to dogs whatsoever. It's a great story, though. Hound Tor is also believed to be the inspiration behind Sir Arthur Conan Doyle's book *The Hound of the Baskervilles*. But what Hound Tor should arguably be most famous for, is the brilliantly named fast-food van located in the car park – The Hound of the Basket Meals.

As groups of walkers headed up towards Hound Tor, Nick and I pedalled off in the opposite direction. Shortly after leaving the car park, we passed a small familiar-looking grass mound by the roadside topped with what looked like a headstone adorned with flowers.

'What was that?' I shouted to Nick as he turned a corner and began belting down a narrow track.

'JAY'S GRAVE!' he shouted.

I had read and seen pictures of the legend of Jay's Grave, but this was the first time I had seen it for real. Jay's Grave has a prominent place in Dartmoor legend and folklore. It is believed to be the final resting place of a suicide victim from the 18th century, named (depending on which story you believe) Kitty Jay, Mary Jay, Betty Kay, Anne Jay or Kay. It is claimed that the three local parishes

– Manaton, Widecombe-in-the-Moor and North Bovey – all refused to bury her in consecrated ground because she had taken her own life. She was buried at an intersection of the roads between the parishes instead.

The stories surrounding the grave have changed many times over the years, but fascination in the spot continues. For decades, fresh flowers have been regularly left on the grave, yet nobody is ever seen laying them, and nobody admits to being responsible. It is claimed the flowers are being left by spirits and some have even suggested pixies from the nearby wood are involved.

This theory was thrown into question in 2001 during the foot-and-mouth disease outbreak. Most of Dartmoor National Park was closed to members of the public to help prevent the spread, and during this time no flowers were placed at Jay's Grave. But all this proves is that the spirits and pixies were honouring the restrictions too.

I turned left and followed Nick down the track. The first mile or so was amazing and just how I imagined mountain biking on Dartmoor would feel. We were whizzing down narrow trails and bridleways which were either loosely gravelled or soft dirt, none of which were too steep. The uphills were tiring, but with the easy gearing of the mountain bike, they were manageable, and I was just about able to keep up with Nick. This optimism of mine was short-lived.

'This next bit is known as Wrist Breaker Alley,' said Nick, pausing at the top of a steeper downhill section.

'Oh, that's good to know. Thanks.'

The soil had eroded away in places, leaving big, exposed rocks to navigate over and around. Many of them were only possible to cycle between if the pedals were at a certain angle, and others I didn't even attempt to squeeze through, opting to lift my bike over instead.

The path eventually levelled out and I still had both wrists intact. I assumed we must be over the worst of it. Then the path dropped further down into the woods with a series of natural rock steps. I watched in awe as Nick just glided down each one as though he was still cycling along the flat. I took a deep breath and released the brakes. I survived the first couple, pushed my bike down the third one, and then saw Nick waiting for me around a corner so felt an obligation to climb back on.

'Holy shit that looks steep,' I said. 'Do you really expect me to cycle down it?'

'You'll be fine. Just don't use your brakes too much when you go over this one,' he said.

'Brakes? Yeah, who needs brakes?'

I steadied myself a few feet above the step and then allowed the front wheel to go over the edge. As the front wheel hit the ground, I panicked and instinctively squeezed the brakes. I was jolted forwards with the back wheel rising behind me. The saddle was now level with my neck, and it nudged me further forwards so that I landed with my crotch on the handlebar stem. My feet landed on the ground, and I regained my balance so that my legs were still on either side of the bike.

'Arghh...' I groaned.

I looked up, and Nick was standing there sobbing with laughter.

'I told you not to use your brakes,' he said.

'Yeah, it's alright for you. You don't know the concept of fear. And what am I supposed to do when my saddle whacks me in the neck?'

'That's why I've got one of these dropper bad boys,' he said, and pressed a magic button on his handlebars and his saddle disappeared down into the frame.

'That's awesome. Does it come back up again?'

He stood on the pedals to take the weight off the saddle, pressed the button again, and the seat post shot up again.

'That's not fair. I want one of those.'

'That section you just came down is known as the Nutcracker.'

'Very funny!'

'No, it genuinely is, and I'd never known why until I saw the way you landed just then. How are your nuts?'

'My nuts are well and truly cracked. Thanks for asking. But I suppose it's reassuring to know that if it's called the Nutcracker that means I can't be the first person that has happened to.'

'Oh no, definitely not. And you won't be the last.'

After a couple of fun miles winding through thick woodland, we found ourselves out on the open moor once again. It was a stunning day to be out on Dartmoor, and a complete contrast to the relentless rain during the Dartmoor Classic a month earlier. The open moor felt a lot more forgiving for a beginner mountain biker than the rocky, woodland trails. There were far fewer obstacles, the ground was soft and peaty and wrist-breaking and nut-cracking seemed less likely. That was until we passed a sign warning of the danger of hidden mineshafts.

Despite the easier terrain, that didn't stop me from injuring myself again. We were on a fast and winding downhill section and came to a bit where Nick had stopped to wait for me. He had a smile on his face, which seemed to be an indication I was in for a nasty surprise. The grassy trail was bordered on either side by thick gorse bushes, and the path was blocked ahead by a patch of mud and a small, steep mossy mound. I had to make a split-second decision about whether to go through the mud or over the mound.

I chose wrong.

The mound was higher than it first appeared and when my front wheel hit it, almost all of my momentum vanished, and my feet slipped from the pedals. My bike came to a complete standstill, but, with the front wheel halfway up the mound, I could not touch the ground with my feet, my toes dangling aimlessly in mid-air. I toppled slowly sideways and face-planted full on into a gorse bush.

'AGGHHH, SHITTY FUCKING FUCK FUCK!'

I emerged to see Nick doubled over with laughter again. 'I'm sorry,' he said. 'But that was so brilliant to watch. I had a feeling that might happen. Are you ok?'

'Yes, I'm fine thanks. You didn't think to warn me?'

'Sorry.'

'I don't think I'm cut out to be a mountain biker.'

'You're doing fine. I want you to come mountain biking with me every time. It's hilarious watching you.'

'Thanks. I'm glad I'm providing you with entertainment.'

'Seriously, though, I've been mountain biking for years. It does take a bit of practice to get used to handling a bike on this sort of terrain.'

'No shit.'

My confidence improved throughout the day, though, and I learned to accept that sometimes – like Nick said – the safest option is to not use the brakes and let gravity do the work.

We were heading down a steep narrow rocky section and Nick had disappeared out of sight before I had even set off. I was trying to navigate a series of rocky ruts, when I heard a loud popping sound, followed by the noise and sensation of my back tyre squashed flat on the ground. I came to a stop, climbed off my bike, and wheeled it down the track where I eventually met Nick leaning on a farm gate.

'What happened to you this time?' he said.

'Sorry. I've got a puncture. Don't suppose you've got a spare inner tube or repair kit?'

'How have you got a puncture?'

'I don't know. I must have ridden over a thorn or something.'

'But your bike has tubeless tyres.'

'What does that mean?'

'There's no inner tube. The tyre just sits on the rim like a car tyre.'

'But surely they can still puncture?'

'Yes, but those tyres are pretty much bulletproof, and they contain self-sealing gunk that should fix any hole.'

'Oh. Well, it's definitely flat. Sorry.'

Nick walked over to take a look.

'It's not a puncture,' he said. 'You've pulled the bloody tyre clean off the rim. How the hell did you do that?'

'Er... I don't know. I did feel the back wheel slip off one of those ruts.'

'Ah,' he sighed. 'That will have done it, you plonker. You need to either ride in the rut or out of it. Not half in and half out.'

'Oops, sorry. If it's tubeless, can't we just put the tyre back on the rim?'

'Unfortunately not,' he said, and then he explained something about sealant and rims and pressure that I didn't understand. I nodded anyway.

Fortunately, Nick had an inner tube for his bike, which just about fitted into the tubeless tyre, and he pumped it up enough for me to be able to cycle the last few miles back to the van.

Mountain biking with Nick was an awakening. Despite not being particularly fast or strong at cycling, I've always felt like I had fairly adequate bike handling skills. I generally feel confident when out and about and don't get too nervous cycling in heavy traffic. But being on a mountain bike on Dartmoor, I felt like I had just had my training wheels removed for the very first time. We had covered 20 off-road miles, with over 3,500 feet of climbing. I felt utterly exhausted, but despite the multiple crashes and wrecking Nick's bike, I had really enjoyed the day and was eager to do it again. I'm a bit of a wimp, though, and unlikely to ever gain a confidence or ability to rival Nick's. I am also keen to try and keep my nuts uncracked.

# SIX

Earlier in the year, Doug, our former neighbour in Northampton whom we lived next door to for 11 years, was diagnosed with pancreatic cancer. He had successful surgery, followed by a few months of aggressive chemotherapy, and somehow seemed to have defied all odds and was given a good prognosis. I spoke to him regularly on the phone during his chemo and he remained upbeat throughout and played down the severity of what he was going through.

During the school summer holidays, I had not been able to get hold of Doug for a couple of weeks. This was unusual as he was a full-time carer for his wife Christine, and only tended to leave the house for the weekly food shop. Two days before we were due to go on holiday to France, I received a Facebook message from the couple who had bought our old house in Northampton – Doug's new neighbours. They said that Doug had been taken ill and he and Christine were in a care home together.

I phoned the care home on the Friday evening, and they

confirmed Doug was with them. They were not allowed to divulge any information about his condition but also said he wasn't currently well enough to be able to speak to me on the phone. Doug had no family and few close friends, and it was upsetting to think of him and Christine in the care home without any familiar faces coming to visit.

'Do you think we should go up to Northampton?' suggested Rachel.

'I don't know. We are going to France on Sunday, and it would be so awful if something happened while we were away and we didn't get to see him.'

'We could go tomorrow?'

'It would be almost a 10-hour round trip. And it wouldn't be very nice for the kids to see Doug in such a bad way.'

'Maybe you should go on your own?'

'And leave you to do all the holiday packing? That doesn't sound very fair on you.'

'I don't mind at all. The kids can pack their own bags.'

'Ha, yeah. Remember, we tried that on our last holiday to Brean? Leo packed just a pair of pyjamas and a Rubik's Cube for three days.'

'I'll check their bags this time. You should go.'

'Ok, if you're sure you don't mind. I think I will always regret it if I don't.'

The following morning, I left home at 5.00am and was at the care home in Northampton by 9.30am. Doug and

Christine were sharing a large high-ceilinged upstairs room, with enormous windows overlooking the gardens below. Doug was dozing listlessly in a bed in the corner.

His eyes widened when he saw me, and his mouth stretched into a big smile.

'Hey, kiddo. What are you doing here?' he said, but his voice was quiet and strained.

'I came to see you, of course. How are you?'

'I'm not so great, kiddo.' He winced and tried to adjust his posture on the bed. 'I'm in so much pain. How's Rachel and the kids?'

'They are all very well, thanks. They all miss you and send their love. Sorry we couldn't all come.'

'Oh, don't be silly. It's so lovely to see you here. I thought maybe you were on holiday.'

'We are going camping in France. Tomorrow actually.'

'That's nice...' he said, and his eyes began to close. His breathing was heavy, and his face tightened each time he felt pain. 'Promise me you'll tell me all about it when you get back.'

'We will all come and see you in September,' I said.

Doug's cancer had returned, and this time had spread quickly throughout his body. He had been admitted to the care home and told he might only have a few weeks to live. Doug was in his mid-seventies and always so feisty and full of energy, and it was heart-breaking to see him like this. A nurse came in and I asked about Doug's pain. She explained it was normal and that it usually takes a few days for them to get the morphine and painkiller dosages under control to make him comfortable.

While Doug dozed, I sat and chatted to Christine for a while. Having been cared for by Doug for nearly 30 years, she was finding the whole experience very strange now that Doug required more care and attention than she did.

When we told Doug and Christine we were moving to Devon they were devastated. Partly because we had built up such a close friendship and they didn't want us to leave, but also because they had become so attached to Father Dougal – our cat. Our house became more and more noisy as Rachel and I brought three children into our life, so Father Dougal started spending more and more time at their house next door where they renamed him Basil. When we moved to Devon, we decided to leave Basil to live with Doug and Christine in Northampton.

With Doug and Christine now in the care home, Doug's current neighbours sent me a message saying they were temporarily looking after Basil, but Doug had asked if they could arrange for me to collect Basil from Northampton and take him down to live with us in Devon. I didn't think now was the time to discuss Basil with Doug so contacted the neighbours and explained we were going on holiday for a couple of weeks but would come and collect Basil as soon as we were back. They said they were very happy to look after him in the meantime.

As I said goodbye to Doug, he squeezed my hand tightly and smiled, his eyes still closed.

'See you soon, kiddo,' he whispered.

Earlier in the year we bought a new car. When I say new, I mean old. And when I say car, I mean van. We had outgrown our small Citroën and packing a family of five into the car for holidays with all our camping equipment and bikes had become an impossible game of Tetris. I had been eyeing up vans for a while, and when the Citroën's clutch failed the day before we were due to go away for my cousin's 40th birthday, and with no time to get it fixed, Rachel and I made a spontaneous decision and bought a van. Packing for this year's trip to France was a doddle compared to previous holidays. And now, for the first time, there was room for all five of our bikes. We could also take our stand-up-paddleboard and five body boards, adding an additional dimension to our holiday.

Due to a combination of lack of availability, and perhaps over-ambition on my part, we had booked three different campsites for our two-week holiday, which meant we (I) had the joy of pitching and repacking the tent three times during the fortnight. It would have been a lot more arduous if we still had the smaller car.

As with my preparation before my first Dart 10k swim two years previously, I had good intentions of regular swim training sessions while on holiday. But like before, my wetsuit and goggles stayed in the car. The Bantham Swoosh would have to act as my sole training for the upcoming double-Dart. I didn't feel the same sense of nervousness and apprehension as last time. Before my first Dart 10k, I had been overwhelmed by a feeling of fear. A feeling that I was about to take on something far beyond my capabilities. I had completed it once, but there was no possible way for me to know how I would feel undertaking it for a second time the following day. This was an entirely new type of fear for me. But I hoped this fear would subside, the closer I got to the gold swim hat.

We enjoyed an action-packed fortnight of cycling, walking, running, table tennis, paddle boarding, body boarding, water slides and lots of eating and drinking. During the holiday, I spoke to Doug a couple of times on the phone, and he seemed to be feeling more comfortable and sounding quite positive about living in the care home. In early September, we would all be travelling back to Northampton for a friend's birthday weekend, and it was now looking hopeful we would all get another chance to see him.

It had been very hard for us to leave Father Dougal/Basil in Northampton when we moved to Devon. However, we knew it was the right thing to do. With Doug unlikely to return to his house, Father Dougal would now come down to live with us in Devon. We were unsure of how he would feel about relocating. But he was now 15 years old and well into his senior years, and thankfully not the wanderer that he once was.

When we returned from France, I contacted the owners of our old house to arrange the logistics of collecting

Father Dougal. I had a reply later that evening.

*'Hope you had a good holiday. Spoke to Doug today – seems like he's changed his mind and wants Basil to stay here where he knows. We'd be happy to keep him, he's very gentle with the girls and not too much trouble, if that's ok with you?'*

Part of me was disappointed as I had been looking forward to having our old cat back with us. The other part was delighted he would be staying in Northampton where he belonged, and I had half expected – maybe even hoped – that Doug would decide for him to stay where he was. They sent a couple of photos of Father Dougal with their two young daughters in our old living room where he first arrived as a kitten. There was something fitting about him spending the first ten years of his life with us, moving next door with Doug for five years, and then returning to the original house to enjoy his retirement.

I replied saying we were delighted that Basil was going to stay with them.

Another reason we thought Father Dougal would be happier staying in Northampton, was that we had been having an increasing number of discussions in recent months about getting a dog.

The rest of the family had been pestering me for years. In fact, way back in 2013, during my celebrations of obscure holidays in my book *Every Day Is a Holiday*, I celebrated Puppy Day by taking an online quiz to see if I was ready for a dog. The results said:

*You're close, but not quite ready.*

*Getting a dog requires a little more work than you may have expected, but your lifestyle needs only a few minor adjustments before you're truly ready.*

I had used these results as my counter argument for not getting a dog ever since. But that was five years ago, and I was definitely warming to the idea. But was I ready? And had we made the necessary adjustments to our lifestyle? I took the same test again.

*Congratulations! You're ready to adopt a dog.*
*You're clearly aware of the responsibilities that come with having a pet.*
*Now see what dog is right for you.*

I wasn't sure what lifestyle adjustments I had made since last time but having used the results of the online test as justification for not getting a dog for five years, it would have been hypocritical for me to ignore the latest assessment. The search for a dog began.

# SEVEN

The ludicrousness of swimming the Dart 10k twice in one weekend didn't fully dawn on me until I woke early on the Saturday morning. I had been so blinded by the incentive of the gold swim hat that I had not really thought through the practicalities of putting my body through such a horrendous ordeal twice.

I had completed it once, so it seemed logical and straightforward that I could just complete it twice. But on the morning of the first of my two swims, I felt sick with nerves. But this was a different kind of fear than I had last time. I was a better swimmer now than when I took part in the event before, so I knew I should be able to at least complete Saturday's swim. It was the prospect of Sunday's swim that was already filling me with dread. As well as Emily and me, we had heard that there were a handful of other swimmers who were also swimming it twice. They are referred to by the Outdoor Swimming Society as double-darters or double-dippers. I wondered if perhaps double dickheads was a more appropriate title.

As I pulled into the car park in a field high above the swim's finish in Dittisham, where swimmers would catch a bus to the start in Totnes, I looked down the hill to the mighty River Dart snaking through the valley below. From my vantage point, it looked serene and tranquil, and I felt strangely privileged to have the opportunity to swim down its course. I took a deep breath to try and make the most of this rare moment of swimming associated positivity. At that exact moment, as if a stark warning from some evil higher power, the 'check engine' warning light flashed brightly on my van's dashboard indicating a fault. My heart sank. I parked up and switched the engine off and on again, hoping the light would miraculously disappear.

It didn't.

I swore loudly at the van and kicked the underneath of the footwell which also strangely didn't fix the problem.

*'Perhaps it just needs some time? Hopefully, it will have fixed itself by the end of the swim,'* I thought to myself as I walked to the bus stop. I was approached by a marshal looking purposeful.

'I know you!' he said.

I looked at him and smiled. I'm often not great at remembering names but I'm usually pretty good at remembering faces. But he didn't look familiar, and he clocked my confusion.

'Don't worry. You don't know me. You're an author, aren't you? George Mahood?'

'Hi, yes I am.'

Being a self-published author, writing obscure travel and adventure books, doesn't result in any level of fame or fortune. I often don't get recognised by friends and family, so it is incredibly rare for me to be recognised by a reader.

'I'm Jon. I'm a big fan. It's really great to meet you. I think I've read nearly all of your books.'

'Aw, thanks. It's really great to meet you too, Jon. Thanks for reading my books. Are you swimming today or just marshalling?'

'Marshalling today and then swimming tomorrow. It will be my first time. You did it a couple of years ago, didn't you?'

'Yes. This will be my second time. I'm swimming tomorrow as well.'

'Tomorrow? And today? That's crazy!'

'I'm shitting myself.'

Jon then told me about his own personal swim challenge which he was midway through, where he was attempting to swim every single day for 50 days in the lead up to his 50th birthday.

'See, to me that seems crazier,' I said. 'On Monday when all this is over, you'll have to go swimming again the next day, and the next day, and the next day. When I get to Monday, I'll probably choose never to swim again.'

'Ha, fair point.'

I wished Jon luck and boarded the waiting bus. This time swimmers could take advantage of a bag drop at the start and so I wasn't wearing my wetsuit. Which was a relief, because five minutes into the 20-minute journey, the bus came to a standstill. A large section of tree had fallen and was blocking the entire road. The bus driver explained how a tractor pulling a high trailer had clipped the tree as it passed and torn it down without even noticing.

By this point, traffic was backed up behind us. The bus driver reported the incident on his radio but was advised it might be a long wait before the tree could be cleared. There were no alternative routes to Totnes along the narrow Devon lanes that would be suitable for a full-length bus. It was looking extremely likely that we would miss the swim start. There would be no option to delay the event because it was dependent on time and tide, which wait for no man.

'I reckon we can all move it!' proclaimed a woman in front of me.

There were a few chuckles from other swimmers, assuming she was joking, but there were some enthusiastic responses too.

'Yeah, there's about thirty of us here,' said the man in the seat opposite. 'How heavy can it be?'

I looked at the tree. It looked pretty fucking heavy to me. But it was definitely worth a try.

The driver opened the door and almost all of us climbed off the bus. A few people started randomly prodding at the trunk, hoping the tree would effortlessly roll off the road. Unsurprisingly, it didn't budge.

Someone took charge and we established a more

organised approach, with some people pushing from one side and others pulling at branches from the other. After a few minutes trying various techniques, we got a bit of momentum together and the tree began to slowly move. It was far too big and the hedgerow at the roadside too thick for us to remove it completely, but after we got the main trunk running parallel to the road, we were able to snap and bend the rest of the protruding branches so that there was just enough space for vehicles to squeeze through one at a time. There was a collective cheer and high-fives from all involved. It was an exciting display of team spirit and for the first time I actually felt a tiny bit excited about the Dart 10k. We were all in this together. I just hoped these 30 other swimmers would help push and pull me down the river, too.

Minutes after arriving at the start, I bumped into Emily and a group of her swimming friends from Northamptonshire. Some were swimming on the Saturday, others swimming on the Sunday, some were volunteering, and some had just come to spectate.

'I haven't yet told these guys I am swimming today AND tomorrow,' whispered Emily.

'What? Why not?'

'I thought I would let it be a surprise for them.'

'Do they think you are swimming today or tomorrow?'

'Tomorrow.'

'Er... Emily, you are wearing a wetsuit now. Won't that

give the game away?'

'I've told them I am going to be event-support in a kayak today.'

'Ha, I love it.'

Emily introduced me to all of her friends and then one of them approached her with a bottle of factor 50 sunscreen.

'Emily, it's going to be really hot today. You'll definitely need lots of this if you're sitting in a kayak all day. Especially with the sun reflecting back off the water.'

'Thanks, good point!' said Emily, looking at me and trying not to laugh. The friend lingered next to her, obviously waiting to have her sunscreen back, so Emily squeezed some into her hand and began smearing it over her face.

'You missed a bit on your nose,' I said. 'You don't want to burn. I would put a bit more on if I were you.'

'He's right. It's going to be boiling,' said the friend. 'You should definitely put more on.'

'Thanks George,' said Emily, smearing another coat of factor 50 all over her face.

I met Matt and Charlie before the start too. They were already wearing their gold swim hats, which are presented to swimmers on the morning of their third swim.

'Wow, look at you two!' I said. 'LOVE the hats!'

'It feels a bit wrong to be wearing them before we've actually finished our third swim,' said Matt.

'No, you deserve to be wearing them now. Make the most of it.'

'I still can't believe you're doing it today and tomorrow,' said Charlie.

'I'm trying not to think about tomorrow. I've got to get today out of the way first.'

I had initially hoped that Matt and Charlie were going to be swimming on the Sunday so that we could all get our gold hats at the same time. But having signed up for three consecutive years, they deserved theirs much more than I did. It was only fair for Matt and Charlie to have a day of bragging rights in their gold hats before I too would hopefully join them.

We were told to gather for our briefing, so Emily pretended to go off to her kayak rendezvous point, before sneaking into the 'leisurely wave' starting pen next to me. She received some odd looks from other swimmers, wondering why someone who was going to have their face underwater for the next three hours would be covered in so much sunscreen.

A few years previously, and unable to swim, Emily signed up for Ironman Frankfurt. She took on weeks of intensive swimming lessons and successfully completed the 2.4-mile swim leg, being last out of the water. Due to a combination of heat exhaustion, two punctures, the harsh German 15-hour cut-off time, and having only recently had a baby, Emily was pulled out of the Ironman towards the end of the 112-mile bike leg. Undeterred, she successfully conquered Ironman Vichy with me the following year. Since then, Emily has been keen to explore other options within triathlon and somehow ended up becoming a guide for a blind triathlete.

Rachel and I took the kids to the Olympic stadium to watch the World Para Athletics Championships in 2017. It was astonishing to watch the patience and dedication of the blind runners and their guides competing at such a high standard out on the track. But imagine the patience, dedication and bravery needed to be a blind triathlete, or the guide for a blind triathlete? For the triathlon swim, both guide and athlete are tethered together, and the guide's role is to make sure their companion stays on course. The bike leg is done on a tandem (tethering two bikes together is unlikely to end well) with the guide sitting at the front (because it makes guiding easier if you can see the road rather than just your partner's backside). Not only does the guide have to cycle every inch of the course, but they also have to provide a continuous commentary of the surroundings, giving cues about the approaching terrain and gradient. The run leg of any triathlon is really tough, with your legs feeling completely alien and unfamiliar after being on the bike. The bravery and trust required from blind athletes is phenomenal. And for Emily, and other triathlete guides, not only do you have your own legs to worry about during the run, but you also have the responsibility of safely guiding your partner around the course too. I had watched videos of Emily and her partner competing in triathlons and they were both equally inspiring.

As we stood waiting for the swim to start, I experienced very different emotions to my first Dart 10k. There was lots of chatter going on amongst swimmers all around us (not all about Emily's sunscreen) and many of them were first timers. You could sense the swirling mixture of fear, excitement and nausea. I didn't have the same fear of the unknown that I had experienced last time. It was more just a sense of foreboding and dread, of knowing what I was going to have to go through. Twice. But as we waded out into the river, I did also feel very fortunate that I was in a position to even contemplate swimming 10k for a second time.

'Good luck, Emily,' I said. 'Try not to get too sunburnt underwater.'

'Ha, thanks. See you at the finish.'

The first mile of the swim felt a lot easier than my previous attempt. I was slightly better prepared this year and the early signs suggested that my regular visits to the pool with Rachel had paid off. I kept wondering if Rachel would enjoy the Dart 10k. She had absolutely loved the Bantham Swoosh, but that had almost been a two-hour sightseeing tour. There was no chance of any underwater viewing in the murky Dart, but I realised I already missed swimming with Rachel.

What got me through my first Dart 10k two years earlier was knowing it would soon all be over. I knew it would not be too long before I was out of the water and could choose never to swim again if I wanted to. This time it was different. There was a constant nagging feeling in the back of my mind that I was going to have to do this all again tomorrow. In 24 hours' time, I would swim along this exact same stretch of riverbank. The longer the swim went on, the more demoralising it became, and the moment of positivity I had briefly felt at the start had quickly drifted off with the current.

But the primary reason for my negative mindset – of which I am embarrassed to even mention here – and an issue that did not fully leave my thoughts for the entire duration of the swim, was my van's 'check engine' light. *What did the warning light mean? How bad was the fault? Would we be able to afford to have it fixed? Would I even be able to get home after the swim?* My GPS watch had never recovered from the soaking it received in the Dartmoor Classic, and I had been debating treating myself to a new watch. A new watch that was so fancy and state-of-the-art I would even be able to use it while swimming. Or even on Dartmoor in the rain! But now a potentially very costly problem with the van would mean a new watch was out of the question. It was something that was completely beyond my control, and I should have been able to ignore it, but different potential scenarios of car diagnoses swirled around my mind for those final few miles, making an already challenging swim even more tortuous.

I knew that Matt and Charlie would most likely be at the finish already, prancing around in their gold hats. Tomorrow, I too could prance around in mine. Before that, however, I would have to go through all of this again. *Would I be able to? Is it worth it? Do I even want the gold swim hat that much?*

The finish line eventually came into view, and I made the final few strokes until I was able to stand up and stagger out of the river. Rachel and the kids had other plans for the day, so I emerged from the river without anyone to greet me. The marshals had offered hugs to all the soggy swimmers at the end of my first Dart 10k, but they seemed to have dispensed with them this time, which was a shame, because I felt like I needed one more than ever.

I was handed a hot chocolate in a lovely commemorative china mug, and I went and found Matt and Charlie who had finished ten minutes before me and were already tucking into a giant burrito. I congratulated them both on their three Dart 10ks, and they wished me luck for my final one the following day.

'Are you going to do it again next year?' I asked.

'No chance!' said Matt. 'I only did it three times for the gold hat.'

'Have you not heard about the new rainbow swim hat they are offering to those that do it five times?'

A look of panic crossed Matt and Charlie's faces.

'Are you serious? A rainbow swim hat?' said Charlie.

'No, I'm just kidding. Well, they better not introduce a new bloody hat.'

I queued for a burrito, and it was so good that I almost looked forward to coming back the next day for another.

I looked around for Emily but couldn't find her. She should have finished before me, so I headed back up the hill to the car park. I called her later and she told me she had met a couple of ladies during the swim who were struggling, so ended up swimming with them the whole way. Thankfully, she didn't get sunburnt.

I bumped into my new reader friend Jon in the car park. It felt like a very long time since I had seen him earlier that morning. Since then, I had helped move a tree, swam 10k, and eaten the world's biggest burrito.

'How was it?' he asked.

'Pretty horrendous, as expected,' I said. 'How has your day been?'

'Fairly dull. I would have much rather been in the water.'

'You'll get your chance tomorrow. Where are you going to do your swim today for your 50-day swim challenge?'

'I'm heading to the pool in Totnes after I've finished my shift here.'

He offered me one of his homemade cookies, which I gladly accepted, and I told him I would look out for him before Sunday's swim.

I took a deep breath and turned the key in the van's ignition. The 'check engine' light was still there. But the van sounded fine, so I decided to try to ignore it until after the weekend.

The following morning, I parked in Dittisham again, and, with a strange sense of déjà vu, boarded the bus. I met Jon again, this time as a swimmer rather than a marshal, and we chatted for the 20-minute journey.

Emily and her friends were already at the start, and she told me how some of her friends had been very slow to realise she was swimming it twice. The previous day, one of them even took a photo of Emily emerging from the river at the finish but assumed she had ended up in the water after a kayak mishap, rather than a 10k swim. It wasn't until they had seen her sipping hot chocolate afterwards and noticed the goggles and swim hat on her head that the penny finally dropped.

I went up to the registration desk as I had done on the Saturday, gave them my name and they handed me an envelope which would contain my coveted prize. My precious. My gold swim hat.

I tore open the envelope, put my hand inside, enjoying the feel of the soft latex on my fingers a bit too much, but when I pulled my hand out, I was clutching a yellow swim hat.

'Excuse me,' I said to the lady behind the desk, trying not to sound too over-dramatic. 'I think there's been some sort of mix-up. Today is my third Dart swim, so I think I should get a gold hat.'

'Oh, sorry about that. Let me just check the gold hat list for you. What is your name?'

I gave my name again and she scanned down a printed paper spreadsheet a few times.

'I'm sorry, your name doesn't seem to be on the list. Have you done it the last three years?'

'No, my first one was two years ago and my second one was yesterday.'

'Ah, ok. That might be why you didn't make it onto the gold hat list before the weekend. I don't know if we have any spares, I'm afraid. I'll have a quick look for you.'

She walked over to a big box of assorted bits and pieces and began rootling through.

'Oh, it really doesn't matter,' I said coyly, trying to play it cool. 'I can just wear the yellow one.'

But it did matter. It mattered a lot. The gold hat was the only reason I had signed up for my second and third swims. Imagine the smile on Matt and Charlie's faces if I swam it three times and didn't even get a gold hat.

'No, there doesn't seem to be any... Oh, what's this? Hooray, a gold hat! There you go!'

'Oh wow, that's amazing,' I squealed, unable to contain my excitement. 'Thank you SO much.'

'You're very welcome. Good luck!'

I joined the others out on the grass and put my wetsuit on. Emily and I both pulled our gold hats on at the same time.

'How do I look?' said Emily. 'Does it suit me?'

'You look great. You look like a much better swimmer than when you were wearing the yellow hat yesterday. Although maybe that was all the sunscreen you were wearing.'

As mentioned before, these gold hats are identical in every way to the coloured swim hats from all the other swim waves. They are just a slightly gold colour. However, the simple act of putting on the gold hat had a strange symbolic effect for both Emily and me. Both complete novice swimmers until relatively recently, we were about to swim our third 10k, and our second in two days. We had looked on in awe at the veteran gold-hatted swimmers during previous swims. Now we had joined them. I felt a little fraudulent considering I still couldn't swim front crawl for any length of time without stopping, but the beauty of the gold hat was that it was not prejudiced against speed or style.

I had hoped my third (and definitely final) Dart 10k would feel easier, knowing I would never have to do it again. But the physical exertion from the day before had taken its toll, and my body protested from the first stroke. My shoulders ached with every turn and my arms felt like they had tripled in weight. I was in no rush, though, so took it nice and easy, reminding myself that every stroke was taking me closer to the finish.

By the time I reached the first feed station after about

4k, I felt extremely light-headed. I had been feeling sick with nerves since I woke up and had forced down a banana for breakfast and eaten nothing else. I drank some water and ate some Jelly Babies and flapjack, and then swam breaststroke for a few minutes, hoping that the sugar would work its magic. I soon felt a little more human, so put my head down and continued swimming.

As we passed the halfway point, I heard someone call my name. I looked to my left and saw Jon swimming alongside me.

'Hey Jon. How the hell did you recognise me while swimming?' I asked.

'Your gold swim hat, of course. It suits you. I'm a little envious.'

Jon had started in one of the faster swim waves much later than me, so was doing really well to have caught me up by halfway. He was looking strong and was enjoying the swim immensely, so after chatting together briefly, I wished him luck and told him to go ahead.

As Jon swam off into the distance, I suddenly became overwhelmed once again with the occasion. I knew now there was a very good chance I would complete the swim, but I still had 5k to go, and the thought of swimming 3.1 miles when my body felt as broken as it did was terrifying.

Half a kilometre later, I heard the unmistakable shout of Emily calling my name from behind.

'Emily! What are you doing? I thought you would be ahead of me.'

'No, I'm just plodding along. How are you doing?'

'Not good. I'm feeling completely wrecked and I don't know if I can swim another 5k.'

'Of course you can. It'll be over in no time.'

'I honestly don't know if I can make it.'

'You will. Let's just take it section by section. Right, you see that blue boat up ahead?'

'Yes.'

'You're going to swim with me to that blue boat, ok?'

'Ok, I'll try.'

We reached the blue boat and then took it steady with a few minutes of breaststroke.

During the final 5k of my Ironman run, I came across Emily who was down to a slow walk and really struggling. She still had over 15k of her run remaining and was in real danger of missing the strict cut-off. We ran together for those 5k, and I tried to offer words of encouragement to keep her moving, in the hope she would continue on and finish her final lap inside the required time. Now it was Emily's turn to coax me through the final kilometres.

We swam the remaining 4.5k together. Our swimming styles could not have been more different, but we seemed to match each other's speed exactly. With no rush to get to the finish, we both alternated stints of front crawl and breaststroke, during which time we chatted away like we were standing on dry land. Emily spent a good chunk of the time trying to convince me to swim the 11-mile long Lake Windermere (England's largest natural lake); a swim that she had completed the previous year.

'You haven't picked the best time to try and convince me to swim nearly twice the distance of a swim I am struggling to finish.'

'Yes, but soon you will have finished this. 11 miles is just more of the same.'

'I don't want more of the same if it's the same as this.'

'But you've got your gold hat now. That means it's time to step up a level. It's time to take on Windermere.'

'After this is over, I am going to burn my wetsuit and goggles.'

'Ha, no you won't. You'll relent eventually. Just you wait.'

Our three combined Dart 10k swims totalled 30k (in case you struggle with maths), which is over 18.5 miles. But it was not until those last couple of miles that I was able to fully enjoy it. It was partly the distraction of chatting to Emily, but also because of the shared sense of achievement we were both feeling. Despite every bit of my body being desperate for the suffering to end, I also wanted to eke out the moment for a little longer, unashamedly proud that we were both now fully deserving of our gold hats.

As my feet made contact with the muddy riverbed, I became a little choked up as I was hit by the realisation of what we had achieved. Completing the swim once had seemed impossible. To have finished it three times just didn't feel real. Goggles and a wet face are a very effective way of hiding the tears.

Rachel and the kids had come to the finish to surprise me, and although I had told them not to, I don't think I would have forgiven them if they hadn't. I was delighted to give them all a big hug on the riverbank. The pleasure was not reciprocated.

'I've just been chatting to one of the Dart 10k staff,' said Emily, as I took a bite of my second epic burrito in two days. 'He told us to go to the Race HQ tent to collect our gift.'

'Gift? What gift?'

'I don't know. Let's go and find out.'

Double-dippers, double-darters or double-dickheads were allowed access to the VIP marquee where we could help ourselves to glasses of champagne and a small buffet. The Outdoor Swimming Society man Emily had chatted to searched through a cardboard box and pulled out a framed certificate congratulating Emily on completing the Dart 10k twice in one weekend.

'Wow, that's lovely. What a nice idea,' I said.

'And what did you say your name was again?' said the OSS man.

'George Mahood.'

He began searching through the box again.

And then again.

'Hmmm, I can't seem to find yours, George.'

'Don't worry. My name wasn't on the gold hat list this

morning, so I probably won't have been picked up as a double-dipper.'

'I'm sure we'll be able to sort something for you,' he said.

He pulled out a framed certificate and handed it to me.

'Here, have this one.'

'Err, thanks. But this one says Adam. I think Adam might be disappointed if I take his certificate.'

'No, it's fine. I know Adam. He won't mind at all. And I think he's gone home already.'

'Thanks, but I honestly don't mind not having a certificate. I wasn't expecting one. And having one with someone else's name on might be a bit weird.'

'Fair enough, I suppose it's a bit like '*here's what you could have won*'. I can ask the team to make a proper one and have it sent to you.'

'That's really kind, but the gold swim hat is honestly all I need. Thank you.'

I went and found the rest of my family, and we said goodbye to Emily. I knew it wouldn't be too long before we saw each other again at some crazy challenge.

It's a long steep uphill climb from Dittisham to the parking field, and with 20k of swimming completed within the previous 28 hours, it felt significantly steeper than usual. We passed a line of swimmers waiting for the bus to take them back to Totnes and I watched as a weary-legged woman sat down on the roadside. As she did so, the carrier bag she was holding made heavy contact with the ground. There was a smashing sound from within the bag and she reached in and pulled out a broken half of her commemorative Dart 10k mug. She looked distraught. I felt distraught for her. It was only a mug. But it was also so much more than that. It was a reminder of what we had all been through and what we had accomplished.

It wasn't until we reached the car park at the top of the hill that I remembered I had two mugs – one from each swim. I could have given her one of mine. I should have given her one of mine. If my muddled brain had reminded me in time. I considered walking back down the hill to offer her one, but then convinced myself that it was too late, and her bus would have already left. To be completely honest, I also couldn't face walking that bloody hill again. I felt so selfish and annoyed with myself for not acting sooner. To this day, each time I use one of my TWO Dart 10k mugs, my tea has a strong taste of remorse. If you were that swimmer and never got a replacement mug for the 2018 Dart 10k, please get in touch. I have a spare!

I had come a very long way since my days in Stroke Development 4. Swimming the Dart 10k for the first time felt like a special achievement. Doing it twice in one weekend was something I never thought I could ever achieve. I felt immense. I was unstoppable. I could achieve anything I put my mind to now.

And then I turned the ignition on and saw the van's

check engine light, and I came crashing back down to earth.

# EIGHT

With our camping stuff only just sorted and put away from our holiday in France, it was time to reload the van for a weekend camping in Northampton to celebrate the 40th birthday of my friend Damo (who claims his grandma invented Banoffee Pie). I had taken the van to the garage a few days before and the cause of the check engine light was thankfully an easy and relatively inexpensive fix. I could treat myself to that new watch after all.

Damo would be the first of our school friends to turn 40 and he had organised a big camping party in September – known as Damofest – to mark the occasion. The rest of us would be turning 40 within the next year, with mine a little over eight months away. The prospect of turning 40 had always seemed alarming when I was younger, but now that I was approaching that big milestone, it didn't bother me at all.

Rachel felt quite anxious about her 40th, which was two months before mine (as I liked to remind her at every chance I got). Not so much because of the actual age – as she was fitter than she had ever been – but because of the added expectation of how to celebrate such a landmark birthday. Damofest helped ease some of these worries. Rachel and I were in the same school year together and being surrounded by all our old friends, it felt in a way that we could use Damofest to celebrate not just Damo's, but all of our birthdays.

I didn't feel old. If anything, I too was probably fitter than I had ever been. And I felt like I was still improving and had not yet reached my peak. I did, however, feel like when it came to setting myself physical challenges, it was all becoming a little bit samey. For the last few years, I had been signing up to the same handful of events – the Dartmoor Classic, Exeter Marathon, Dart 10k, Cotswold 113, Cornish Marathon and various others. Nine of the first ten marathons I completed were brand new events to me. Only the Cornish marathon – with its lure of a hoodie and Cornish pasty – had I done more than once. I had deliberately chosen new events each time, trying to keep things fresh and interesting. But now I had unintentionally found myself in a bit of a rut, with the same old events now becoming regular fixtures on my calendar.

On one hand, I welcomed the familiarity of taking part in these events multiple times, as the occasion was always less intimidating the second time around. But this familiarity also brought with it a sense of comfort and perhaps ease. I wasn't testing myself, and repeating the same events each year was a cautious and unadventurous option.

I made a deal with myself that I would take a break from the tried and trusted events (with the likely exception of the Cornish Marathon; a new hoodie ensuring the event would feel unique each year). This didn't mean I was taking a break from physical challenges. Far from it. I still wanted to challenge myself and test my capabilities. But I wanted to expand my horizons with different adventures and less familiar experiences.

While back in Northamptonshire, we all went to visit Doug and Christine in their care home. It had been almost a year since Rachel and the kids had last seen Doug, and I warned them how different he would look. It had been over a month since my last visit, so there was a good chance he would have deteriorated further since I last saw him, too.

We signed in at reception and walked up the creaky old staircase of the former manor house to Doug and Christine's room. As we reached the top of the stairs, I could already hear Doug laughing and joking with a nurse. He turned as I entered the room.

'HEEEY, KIDDO!' he shouted. 'Wow, what a lovely surprise.'

'Hi Doug. Hi Chris,' I said. 'I've brought the family this time!'

'OH MY, THE WHOLE GANG IS HERE!'

'Hi Doug. Hi Chris,' they all said, and Doug gave

Rachel, Layla, Leo and Kitty each a big hug.

'Oh wow,' he said. 'It's so wonderful to see you all.'

Doug was looking like a different person to when I saw him last. He had lost a bit more weight and was looking a little older, but his spark was well and truly back. He seemed to have more energy and enthusiasm than I'd seen in him before.

'Can I get you guys a drink?' asked the nurse.

*I'll have what Doug's having*, I thought to myself.

Rachel and I declined but she brought the kids each a glass of juice.

We sat in the room with Doug and Chris for a while, but Doug seemed too excited to be contained inside.

'It's such a beautiful day,' I said, looking out of the huge windows that overlooked the gardens.

'Come on, let's go outside,' said Doug. 'Will you take me?'

I looked to Rachel.

'Um, yeah I guess so,' she said. 'Is that allowed?'

'Of course it's allowed!' laughed Doug. 'I'm the lord of the manor here. I can do what I like.'

'Is that ok with you, Chris?' I said. 'We won't be long.'

Chris smiled and nodded. She was never too keen on having visitors, so the five of us being in her room was probably a little overwhelming for her.

'I'm going to need a hand,' said Doug, pointing to his wheelchair. 'I'm not great with this thing.'

'Do we have to wheel you down the stairs?' asked

Rachel.

'No, don't be daft! There's a lift. Imagine me bouncing all the way down those stairs in this chair.'

'Phew, I did wonder,' said Rachel. 'That's a relief.'

We wheeled Doug down the corridor and then all squeezed into the tiny elevator together and descended to the ground floor.

'Are they kidnapping you?' said one of the staff as we wheeled Doug towards the door.

'Oh, I wish they would,' laughed Doug.

We all sat together in the sunshine on the terrace outside and told Doug all about our summer holiday, our recent swims and bike rides, and of how well Basil seemed to have settled in with Doug's neighbours. Layla, Leo and Kitty chatted about how they were getting on at school.

'Layla, I can't believe you've started secondary school,' said Doug. 'It seems like only yesterday when you were born.'

Layla and Kitty were both born at home in Northampton, and Doug held them both within an hour of being born. Leo was born in hospital and Doug was one of his very first visitors once we were home.

We also chatted about Northampton Town Football Club's poor start to the football season. After being relegated from League One at the end of the previous campaign, the Cobblers were now languishing near the bottom of League Two. Despite the football results, Doug seemed genuinely happy. Possibly the happiest I had ever seen him. For the past 30 years, he had been a full-time carer to his wife and almost every waking moment had been spent looking after Christine. Now, for the first time, he was the one being looked after.

'To be honest,' he said, 'it's like living in a really posh hotel. I get all my meals cooked for me, cups of tea brought to my room, someone comes and makes the beds, and there's entertainment almost every night. And all the staff and other residents are so lovely.'

'That's so great to hear,' said Rachel. 'And how's Christine doing?'

'She's the same as ever. I think she finds it hard that after all these years of me looking after her that now I'm the ill one. But I think I deserve a bit of looking after, don't you?'

'Of course you do,' I said. 'It's so lovely that you are happy here.'

We didn't go into too much detail about Doug's illness, but we knew – and he knew – that this would likely be the last time we saw him. We had become extremely close to Doug in the 16 years we had known him. Rachel and I moved next door to him and Christine as a childless, petless, unmarried couple. Over the following few years, we married and then added three children and two cats, and the quiet terraced house next to Doug and Christine suddenly became a lot livelier. But Doug loved having us as neighbours and he now felt like part of our family.

'Where have you been, Doug?' said Christine, with a slight tone of anger.

'The lift was broken. We had to wait for an engineer. Didn't we, George?'

'Sorry, what was that, Doug?' I asked, arriving in the room a bit later than the others.

Doug fixed me with a glare.

'The lift, George. It was broken, wasn't it?'

'Oh... yeah, that's right. Very broken. It's all fixed now though.'

Chris seemed to accept the excuse.

'Are you still driving that old Citroën?' asked Doug.

'No! Did we not tell you? We bought a van!'

'A van? Wow! Have you got it here?'

'Yes, you can probably see it from the window.'

I walked over to the window, but the van was just out of sight.

'Will you take me and show me?' asked Doug.

Christine gave a slight grunt of disapproval.

'Please,' he added. 'Just a quick look.'

'Of course!' I said. 'I'll have him back in a few minutes, Chris.'

We all said goodbye to Christine and wheeled Doug back along the corridor, down the elevator and out into the car park.

'Wowwee,' he said. 'It's a beast!'

Layla, Leo and Kitty gave Doug a guided tour of the

van as I wheeled him around the outside in his chair.

'What's your mum like at parking this?' whispered Doug to the kids.

One of the highlights of Doug's day when we were neighbours in Northampton was to stand at his front window and watch Rachel reverse park.

'Pretty bad,' said Layla.

'Hey, I heard that,' laughed Rachel. 'Although, she's right, Doug. I'm not great.'

'Well, I love it. I'm sure you'll all have lots of adventures together in this.'

Rachel, Layla, Leo and Kitty each gave Doug a big hug and a kiss and I wheeled him back up to his room.

'Take care of your lovely family, kiddo. Thanks for coming to visit, it's been so special to see you all.'

'It's been really lovely to see you both too, and it's wonderful to see how happy you are here.'

'Can't complain, kiddo. Can't complain.'

Doug had been given his first ever mobile phone but didn't really know how to use it. I plugged it in next to his bed and gave him a quick tutorial of how to make and receive calls.

During the following six weeks we spoke to him regularly on the phone and he remained positive throughout. I called him a couple of times in late October, and he didn't answer his mobile, so I phoned the care home and asked if it was possible to speak to him.

'He's struggling to speak at the moment, and he's very

tired,' said the member of staff. 'He'll be delighted to know you called though.'

'Could you pass a message onto him from me, please?'

'Of course.'

'Can you tell him the Cobblers just beat Macclesfield 5-0. Matt Crooks scored a hat-trick.'

'I'll pass it on. He'll be delighted to hear that. Thanks.'

We received news the following day that Doug had died peacefully in his sleep.

Having been housebound as a carer for almost thirty years, Doug was always desperate to hear stories of what Rachel and I had been up to and where we had been. He read and enjoyed all of my books and lived all of my adventures vicariously.

It had been three years since my Ironman, and in those intervening years Rachel and I had taken on many different running, cycling and swimming challenges. 2019 was going to be a big year with us both turning 40. But for the first time since before my back surgery, we didn't have a single event or challenge lined up. Having decided to take a break from the same old events, we had not yet replaced them with anything different. Were we giving up simply because we were soon turning 40? Was this an early retirement from sporting challenges? The news of Doug's death made me feel like I was already letting him down.

I needed a new challenge. I needed to head off somewhere, experience something new, challenge myself once again. But I needed a different sort of adventure.

Something that Doug would have loved to hear about. Or something that he would have loved to have taken part in too. It was the end of October, but I was too impatient to wait until spring. I picked up my phone and began googling.

'What are you smiling about?' asked Rachel.

'I've got an idea. Do you want to come on a cycle trip with me to France?'

'France? When?'

'Next week.'

## Author's note

Thank you for choosing to read my book. If you enjoyed it, I would be extremely grateful if you would consider posting a short review on Amazon and help spread the word about my books in any way you can.

You can get in touch via social media:
**www.facebook.com/georgemahood**
**www.instagram.com/georgemahood**
**www.twitter.com/georgemahood**

Or join my mailing list on my useless website to be the first to hear about new releases.
**www.georgemahood.com**
Signed copies of all of my books are available in my website's 'shop'.

*Did Not Finish* is a series of books. Please read on…

## Book Five...

*Did Not Enter* – book five in the *DNF* series – is available to order on Amazon.

Here is the blurb...

Soon to turn 40, George and Rachel decide to take a break from the usual organised events, instead seeking adventure elsewhere.
Two different cycling adventures in France follow. One a race against time. The other a race against wine.
To celebrate his milestone birthday, George and Rachel take on their longest run yet – 40 miles along Britain's oldest road.
There's yoga, a funeral, self-imposed running and swimming challenges, and a marathon with the hangover from hell.
A new hairy, four-legged addition to the Mahood family brings more fun, adventure... and rosettes.

*Did Not Finish is a series of books about George and his family's adventures in running, cycling and swimming. From ultramarathons to triathlons, 10k swims to European cycling adventures, George promises fun and laughter every step, pedal, and paddle of the way.*

BOOK FIVE IN THE DNF SERIES

# DID NOT ENTER

MISADVENTURES IN RUNNING CYCLING AND SWIMMING

## GEORGE MAHOOD

# Acknowledgments

First thanks go to all the organisers, marshals and volunteers for putting on these races. Many of them stand outside all day in horrendous conditions, often with no reward or incentive other than the satisfaction of being a part of the event. And perhaps the joy of watching us suffer.

Special thanks to our family and friends who regularly step in to help with childcare while Rachel and I are taking part in these events.

Rachel's editing job for these books was not as scrupulous as usual, which she claimed was because she enjoyed them so much. I think that is only because she features so prominently in them. She would often write 'LOL' in the margin, even though she had been sitting next to me while reading and hadn't made a murmur. Anyway, thank you for lolling (internally).

Becky Beer was as ruthless as ever with the red pen during her proofreading. That's a compliment. Thank you! Please check out her Bookaholic Bex blog (www.bookaholicbex.wordpress.com) and Facebook page.

Thanks to Robin Hommel and Miriam for additional proofreading and feedback.

Thanks to all our friends who have taken part in these challenges and adventures with us. It is always reassuring to not be the only ones with a ridiculously stupid concept of 'fun'.

Thanks to Rachel… AGAIN (she's even got a starring role in the acknowledgements) for reluctantly agreeing to take part in many of these events with me. We are not always perfect running. cycling, swimming partners, but I wouldn't want it any other way.

Thanks to Layla, Leo and Kitty for putting up with your annoying parents and for continuing to inspire and amuse us. Hopefully one day you will look back and be glad we dragged you out on all these walks.

Thanks to my mum and dad for dragging me out on all those walks when I was younger. I didn't appreciate it at the time, but I do now.

Lastly, thanks to you for reading this series. The idea that people enjoy reading about random things I get up to still feels very bizarre to me, but I'm always honoured and grateful.

Big love.

## Also by George Mahood

**Free Country:** A Penniless Adventure the Length of Britain

**Every Day Is a Holiday**

**Life's a Beach**

**Operation Ironman:** One Man's Four Month Journey from Hospital Bed to Ironman Triathlon

**Not Tonight, Josephine:** A Road Trip Through Small-Town America

**Travels with Rachel:** In Search of South America

**How Not to Get Married:** A no-nonsense guide to weddings… from a photographer who has seen it ALL

(available in paperback, Kindle and audiobook)

Did Not Sink

George Mahood